D0778593

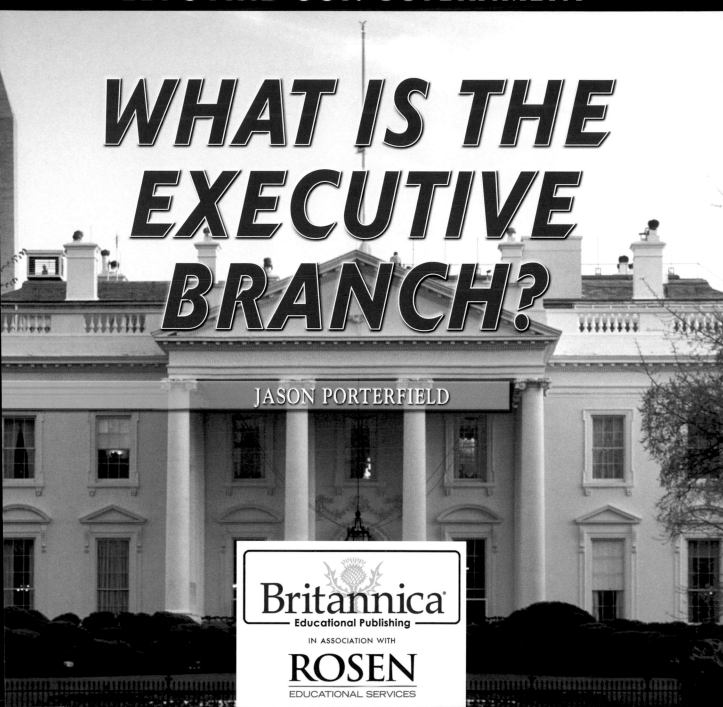

WHAT IS THE EXECUTIVE BRANCH?

JASON PORTERFIELD

Britannica
Educational Publishing

IN ASSOCIATION WITH

ROSEN
EDUCATIONAL SERVICES

Published in 2016 by Britannica Educational Publishing (a trademark of Encyclopædia Britannica, Inc.) in association with The Rosen Publishing Group, Inc.
29 East 21st Street, New York, NY 10010

Distributed exclusively by Rosen Publishing.

To see additional Britannica Educational Publishing titles, go to rosenpublishing.com.

First Edition

Britannica Educational Publishing
J.E. Luebering: Director, Core Reference Group
Mary Rose McCudden: Editor, Britannica Student Encyclopedia

Rosen Publishing
Hope Lourie Killcoyne: Executive Editor
Kathy Kuhtz Campbell: Senior Editor
Nelson Sá: Art Director
Danijah Brevard: Designer
Cindy Reiman: Photography Manager
Karen Huang: Photo Researcher

Library of Congress Cataloging-in-Publication Data

Porterfield, Jason.
What is the executive branch?/Jason Porterfield.
        pages cm.—(Let's find out! government)
Includes bibliographical references and index.
ISBN 978-1-62275-922-4 (library bound)—ISBN 978-1-62275-927-9 (pbk.)—ISBN 978-1-62275-929-3 (6-pack)
1. Executive departments—United States—Juvenile literature. 2. Presidents—United States—Juvenile literature.
3. Cabinet officers—United States—Juvenile literature. I. Title.
JK501.P67 2016
351.73—dc23

2014037154

Manufactured in the United States of America

Photo credits: Cover, interior pages background image Richard Nowitz/National Geographic Image Collection/Getty Images; pp. 4, 19 Bloomberg/Getty Images; p. 5 National Archives, Washington, D.C.; p. 6 Heritage Images/Hulton Archive/Getty Images; p. 7 DEA Picture Library/De Agostini/Getty Images; p. 8 Saul Loeb/AFP/Getty Images; pp. 9, 12, 24, 26 Library of Congress Prints and Photographs Division; pp. 10, 18, 23 Official White House Photo by Pete Souza; p. 11 Pool/Getty Images; p. 13 Nicholas Kamm/AFP/Getty Images; p. 14 Frederic J. Brown/AFP/Getty Images; p. 15 Matthew Healey/UPI/Landov; p. 16 LBJ Library; pp. 17, 20, 21, 22, 29 © AP Images; p. 25 AFP/Getty Images; p. 27 FDR Presidential Library & Museum, CC BY 2.0; p. 28 The White House/Getty Images.

CONTENTS

THE BRANCHES OF GOVERNMENT

Countries around the world are led by governments. A government makes important decisions that affect the lives of its people. It guards them against outside enemies and keeps order within the country. It provides services to its people. States and cities also have governments.

The president of the United States is in charge of the executive branch.

The United States is a **representative democracy** that is made up of three parts, or branches. These are the executive branch, the legislative branch, and the judicial branch. Each branch's powers are given by the United States Constitution. The legislative branch makes laws. The judicial branch runs the courts and uses the Constitution and other laws to settle cases. The job of the executive branch is to carry out the laws.

The U.S. Constitution lists the powers of the three branches of government.

Government for the People

The U.S. Constitution sets out the country's most basic laws. All other laws must agree with the U.S. Constitution.

In 1776, 13 colonies in North America declared independence from Great Britain. They fought a war for their independence and then formed the new country of the United States. The

Many people in the 13 colonies considered King George III of Great Britain a cruel and unfair ruler.

It took the work and ideas of many people to write the Constitution.

colonies became states. The newly independent citizens did not want a single leader to rule over them. Many felt that the British king who had ruled over the former colonies was a tyrant who limited their freedom. The new nation's founders wrote the Constitution in 1787. They wanted to protect the rights of the country's citizens.

The founders also wanted to make sure that one branch of government could not become more powerful than the others. They did not want one leader to become as powerful as a king.

> **VOCABULARY**
> A **tyrant** is a ruler who has complete power over a country and who is cruel and unfair.

CHECKS AND BALANCES

According to the Constitution, each branch of government has some power over the others. This is called a system of checks and balances. For example, the leader of the executive branch (the president) gets to appoint, or choose, many government leaders. But part of the legislative branch (the Senate) has the power to reject the president's choices.

The U.S. Senate holds hearings to decide whether people the president selects should be appointed to certain jobs.

Congress can charge the president with breaking the law. This charge is called impeachment. The Senate holds a trial to decide whether or not the president is guilty. A guilty president must resign, or step down. The House of Representatives has impeached two presidents, Andrew Johnson and Bill Clinton, but the Senate found them both not guilty.

COMPARE AND CONTRAST

Each branch of the U.S. government has some say in how the other two branches can act. Compare and contrast this system with one lacking checks and balances. Which is more likely to be governed for the people?

Organizing the Executive Branch

The Constitution describes how the government is organized. The executive branch is headed by the president of the United States.

The president is joined in the executive branch by the vice president and a group of advisers called the cabinet. Each member of the cabinet is in charge of a separate department, such as the Department of

Vice President Joseph Biden speaks with President Barack Obama in the White House.

The president's full cabinet meets regularly to talk about important issues.

Agriculture or Department of Education. Today there are 15 cabinet departments.

Members of the cabinet have to be approved by Congress. The president tries to choose men and women who have experience connected to their departments and who are likely to do a good job.

THINK ABOUT IT

Each state also has an executive branch headed by a governor. Can you name your state's governor?

WHO CAN BE PRESIDENT?

There are not many limits on who can become president. The Constitution says that the president must be at least 35 years old, a natural-born U.S. citizen, and a resident of the United States for at least 14 years.

During the country's early years, only men who owned property could become

At age 42, Theodore Roosevelt was the youngest person ever to become president.

president or even vote. This is no longer the case. Today, almost any American-born man or woman can become president. However, a person who has been proved guilty of a felony, or a very serious crime, cannot be president.

Hillary Clinton ran for president in 2008 and almost became the Democratic Party's nominee, or choice.

THINK ABOUT IT

For many decades, women and minorities did not run for president. They were also kept from voting. How has this changed in recent years?

Becoming President

A president is chosen in an **election** held every four years. There are usually only two, sometimes three, serious candidates in an election. Most voters pick the candidate from the political party they most agree with. The Democratic Party and the Republican Party are the two major political parties in the United States. Political parties are groups of people who usually have similar beliefs about the role of government and how it should be run.

These citizens at a polling place are voting in a presidential election.

Vocabulary

An **election** is the process of choosing someone for public office by voting.

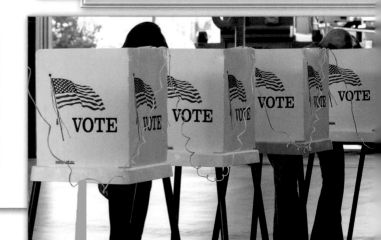

14

The president is not directly elected by individual voters. Instead, a group called the electoral college elects the president and the vice president. Electoral college members usually choose the candidate who won the popular vote in their state. Electoral votes are given to each state based on population.

A candidate can become president without winning the most states. A candidate can even become president without winning the popular vote. This happened most recently in 2000, when George W. Bush lost the popular vote to Al Gore but won the electoral vote.

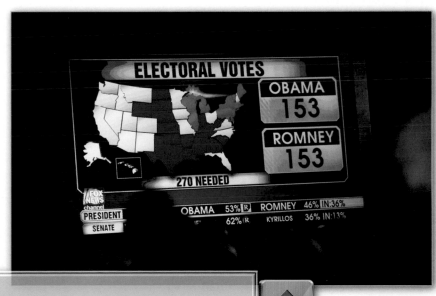

A map shows which candidate gets each state's electoral votes during the 2012 presidential election.

THE VICE PRESIDENT

The president and vice president are elected together. Each candidate for president picks someone to run as vice president. A lot of thought goes into picking the right candidate for vice president. If the president dies or resigns, the vice president becomes president. The vice president has to be prepared to lead the nation.

Vice President Lyndon B. Johnson became president after the death of John F. Kennedy.

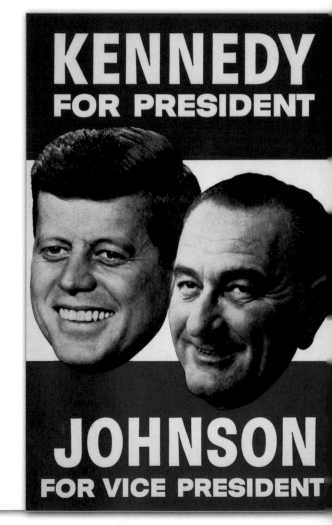

THINK ABOUT IT

Vice presidents often run for president later in their careers. Why would a former vice president make a good president?

The vice president's only real duty is to serve as the president of the Senate. If a Senate vote is tied, the vice president casts the deciding vote. The vice president also leads cabinet meetings if the president is away. Vice presidents do a lot of work with members of Congress to get laws passed and to support the president.

Vice President Dick Cheney *(center)* meets with cabinet members in the Capitol after he cast a tie-breaking vote in the Senate.

Inside the Executive Office

Besides the cabinet, the president has a staff of people who offer help and advice. The White House chief of staff leads this group. The agencies, or departments, in the executive office handle many day-to-day tasks that the president is too busy to take on. These agencies include the Office of Management and Budget, the National Security Council, and several others.

The White House Office is also part of

President Barack Obama meets with the White House chief of staff Denis McDonough.

The White House press secretary gives information to reporters and answers their questions.

COMPARE AND CONTRAST

The members of the cabinet often focus on broad topics. Workers in the executive office usually work out the details of their ideas. How is it useful to have one group working on smaller points?

the executive office. It is made up of the president's personal staff members. This includes advisers, experts, and people who help the president communicate with Congress. The people in the executive office also talk to reporters at press conferences and work with the legislative branch to get laws passed.

CRAFTING POLICY

The president does not have the power to make laws. For a law to be made, a member of Congress has to introduce it as a document called a bill. The president works with the White House Office and the cabinet to make suggestions about the bill. The bill is then crafted by Congress. The two houses of Congress must agree on the bill and vote on it. If the bill is approved, it goes to the president. The president then must decide either to sign

President Obama signs a bill into law after it passed in both houses of Congress.

President George W. Bush explains the reasons why he decided to veto a bill.

the bill or to veto, or block, it. Once it is signed, it becomes law.

The veto is one of the president's most powerful tools for shaping laws. A president can veto any bill. When a bill is vetoed, Congress can start over by making a new bill, or it may try to fix the bill.

> **VOCABULARY**
>
> The **veto** is a power described in the Constitution that allows the president to block bills and other official acts before they become law.

ENUMERATED POWERS

The Constitution grants two kinds of powers to the president. These are called enumerated and implied powers. Enumerated powers are those that are mentioned in the Constitution. They give the president the power to carry out certain duties. These are the powers to veto bills, pardon prisoners, carry out federal laws, and command the nation's military. Enumerated powers also include appointing people to important posts and justices to the Supreme Court. The president

President Gerald Ford issued a pardon for former president Richard Nixon after Nixon stepped down from office.

can also receive representatives from other nations and make treaties.

Appointing Supreme Court justices is a lot like appointing cabinet members. The president wants qualified candidates who will do a good job and who can be approved by Congress. The president often chooses justices who share his or her viewpoints and values. They also should have a solid record for fairness.

President Obama appointed Justice Sonia Sotomayor to the U.S. Supreme Court.

VOCABULARY
Treaties are official agreements that are made between two countries or groups.

Implied Powers

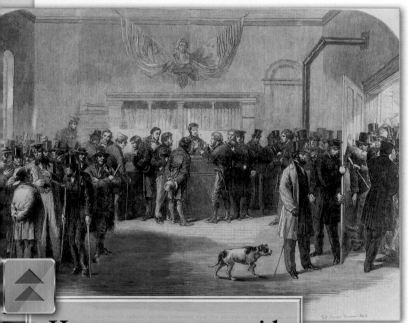

Here, men try to avoid having to become soldiers during the Civil War. President Abraham Lincoln used his implied powers to order men to join the army.

Implied powers are not written in the Constitution. Instead, the wording of the document suggests that they are available to the president. Implied means to express something in an indirect way. Implied powers include organizing the executive branch, making executive orders, and beginning military action.

Executive orders are statements by the president that must be obeyed like laws.

In 1957 the Arkansas governor tried to stop African American students from going to an all-white school in Little Rock. President Dwight Eisenhower used an executive order to open the school to the students.

Presidents can use executive orders to make important decisions without consulting with Congress. Presidents also sometimes issue executive orders to change the way earlier bills are enforced, or made effective. Some presidents have made only a few executive orders. Others have issued thousands.

THINK ABOUT IT

In 1970, President Richard Nixon issued an executive order to establish the Environmental Protection Agency. The agency's job today is to protect the health of people and the environment by enforcing laws passed by Congress. What kind of laws does this agency enforce?

TERM LIMITS

The inauguration ceremony for George Washington's second term as president was held in Philadelphia, Pennsylvania.

There are limits to how long a person can be president. Presidents serve four-year stretches of time called terms. After the first four years, the president can run again or step aside for another candidate to run. Most presidents who complete their first term choose to run again. A

THINK ABOUT IT

The Constitution limits presidents to two terms of office. Why did some lawmakers think it was important to limit the president to eight years in power?

president who runs again and wins is reelected and serves a new term. Presidents can be elected to only two terms. This was not always the case, and several presidents have run for more terms.

Only Franklin D. Roosevelt was ever elected to more than two terms. He was elected to four terms. He was president from 1932 to 1945.

Franklin Roosevelt was sworn in for his fourth term as president in January 1945.

CHANGING OF THE GUARD

When a president's last term is over, the newly elected president, or president-elect, takes office. The president who is leaving often gives advice to the president-elect before handing the office over. The president-elect officially becomes president in a ceremony called the inauguration that takes place on January 20. At the event, the president-elect takes the oath of office from the chief justice of the Supreme Court.

In most cases, the new president hires an entirely new staff of

President George W. Bush met with President-elect Barack Obama before the start of Obama's first term.

VOCABULARY
An **inauguration** is an event that introduces someone into a job or position with a formal ceremony.

advisers. Cabinet members are usually replaced with people who share the new president's ideas and views.

Not many cabinet members go on to serve more than one president, even if they are from the same political party. The new cabinet members must be approved by the Senate in the U.S. Congress.

The new president and vice president will have to come up with their own plans and course of action. They also have to build relationships in Congress. They have four to eight years to work with the other branches of government to keep the country working for the people.

During his second term in office, President Obama gave a speech asking Congress to protect children from being hurt by guns.

GLOSSARY

advisers People who give an opinion or suggestion to someone about what should be done.

appoint To choose someone for a particular job or to give someone a position or duty.

cabinet A group of people who give advice to the leader of a government.

careers Jobs or professions that people do for a long time.

chief of staff A person of high rank who advises a leader (such as the U.S. president) on important matters.

citizens People who legally belong to a country and have the rights and protection of that country.

constitution A system of beliefs and laws by which a country or state is governed.

document An official paper that gives information about something or that is used as proof of something.

interpret To understand (something) in a specified way.

issue To give something to someone in an official way, or to announce something in a public or official way.

judicial branch The part of government that uses the U.S. Constitution and other laws of the U.S. government to settle legal cases.

legislative branch The part of government that has the power to make laws.

military Relating to soldiers or the armed forces (such as the army, navy, marines, and air force).

organized Arranged in a group with leaders and rules for doing or planning things.

pardon To officially say that someone who is guilty of a crime will be allowed to go free and will not be punished.

qualified Having the necessary skill, experience, or knowledge to do a particular job or activity.

security The state of being protected or safe from harm.

surveillance The act of carefully watching someone or something, especially to prevent or detect a crime.

FOR MORE INFORMATION

BOOKS

Bow, James. *What Is the Executive Branch?* New York, NY: Crabtree Publishing, 2013.

Davis, Todd, and Marc Frey. *The New Big Book of U.S. Presidents: Fascinating Facts About Each and Every President, Including an American History Timeline.* Philadelphia, PA: Running Press Kids, 2013.

Jukubiak, David J. *What Does the President Do?* (How Our Government Works). New York, NY: Rosen Publishing, 2010.

Landau, Elaine. *The President, Vice President, and Cabinet: A Look at the Executive Branch.* Minneapolis, MN: Lerner Publications, 2012.

Morey, Allan. *A Timeline History of the Early American Republic.* Minneapolis, MN: Lerner Publications, 2014.

WEBSITES

Because of the changing nature of Internet links, Rosen Publishing has developed an online list of websites related to the subject of this book. This site is updated regularly. Please use this link to access the list:

http://www.rosenlinks.com/LFO/Exec

INDEX